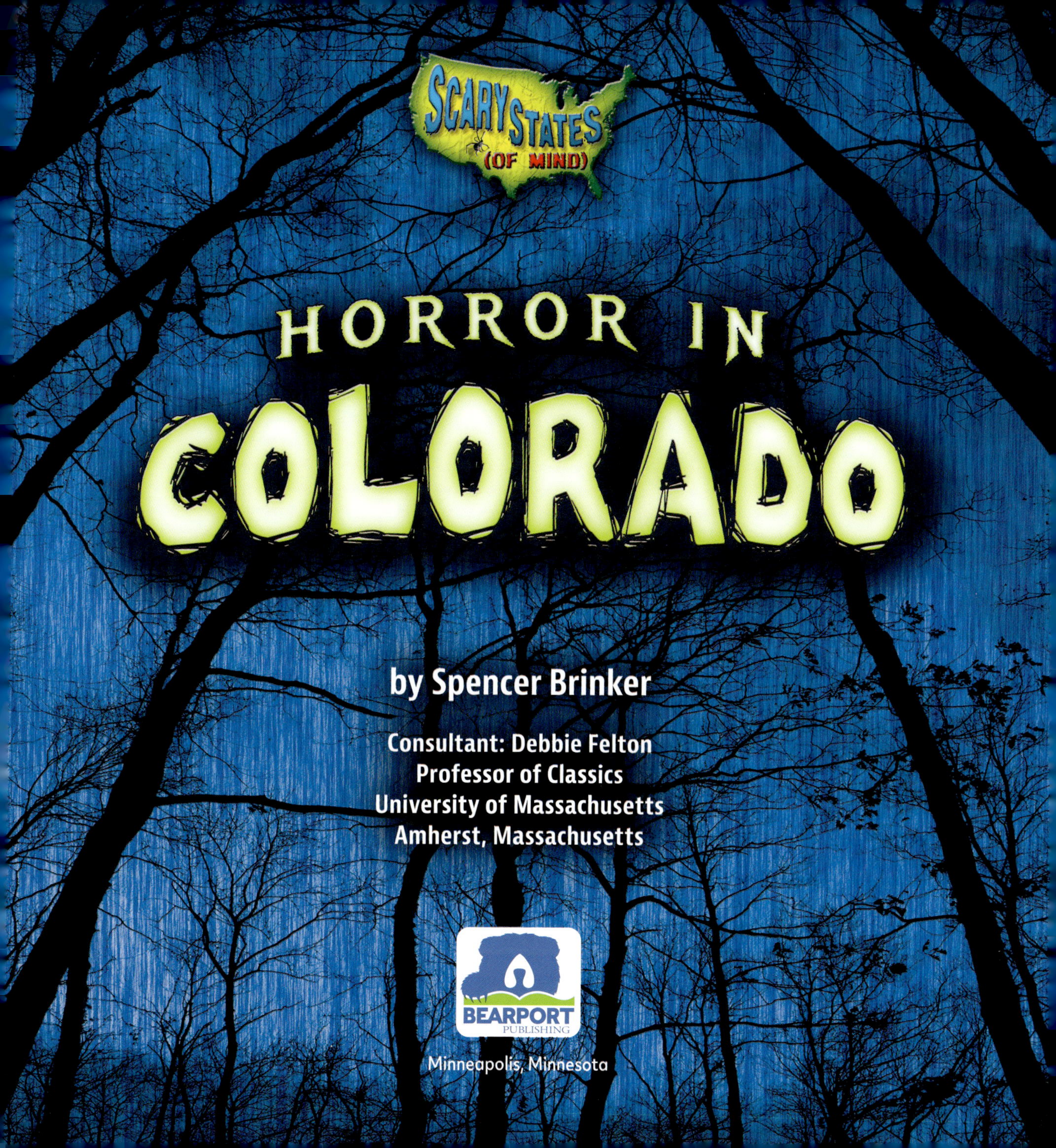


# HORROR IN COLORADO

by Spencer Brinker

Consultant: Debbie Felton
Professor of Classics
University of Massachusetts
Amherst, Massachusetts

BEARPORT
PUBLISHING

Minneapolis, Minnesota

**Credits**

Cover, © Kim Jones, © Hale Kell/Shutterstock, © Aleksandr Denisyuk/Shutterstock, © Kwadrat/Shutterstock, and © ssuaphotos/Shutterstock; 3, Robert Crum; 4-5, © Kim Jones, © LanaG/Shutterstock, © LumineImages/Shutterstock, © Eric Isselee/Shutterstock, and © DarkBird/Shutterstock; 6, Courtesy The Denver Public Library, Western History Collection, [Call z-306]; 7, © jennifer_crowder_artist/Shutterstock; 8, © John Wollwerth/Shutterstock; 9, © RJ Sangosti/Shutterstock; 11, © Plazak/Wikimedia Commons/Creative Commons; 12, © Jeffrey Beall/Wikimedia Commons/Creative Commons; 13, © Janelle Lugge/Shutterstock; 14-15, © Phillip Rubino/Shutterstock; 15, Wikimedia Commons/Public Domain, ; 17, © Kaul Photo and Cinema/Shutterstock; 17 inset, © Moviestore Collection/Shutterstock, ; 19, © Matthew Kiger; 19 inset, Wikimedia Commons/Public Domain; 20, © sutlafk/Shutterstock; 21, © CustomPhotographyDesigns/Shutterstock; 23, © Josh Schutz/Shutterstock; and 24, © bepsy/Shutterstock.

President: Jen Jenson
Director of Product Development: Spencer Brinker
Editor: Allison Juda
Designer: Micah Edel
Cover: Kim Jones

*Library of Congress Cataloging-in-Publication Data*

Names: Brinker, Spencer, author.
Title: Horror in Colorado / by Spencer Brinker.
Description: Minneapolis, Minnesota : Bearport Publishing Company, [2021] | Series: Scary states (of mind) | Includes bibliographical references and index.
Identifiers: LCCN 2020000561 (print) | LCCN 2020000562 (ebook) | ISBN 9781647470715 (library binding) | ISBN 9781647470814 (ebook)
Subjects: LCSH: Haunted places—Colorado—Juvenile literature. | Ghosts—Colorado—Juvenile literature. | Colorado—Miscellanea—Juvenile literature.
Classification: LCC BF1472.U6 B7274 2021 (print) | LCC BF1472.U6 (ebook) | DDC 133.109788—dc23
LC record available at https://lccn.loc.gov/2020000561
LC ebook record available at https://lccn.loc.gov/2020000562



For more information, write to Bearport Publishing, 5357 Penn Avenue South, Minneapolis, MN 55419.

# CONTENTS

# Horror in Colorado

Colorado is known for the tall peaks of its beautiful mountains. It's also famous for its ghosts and spirits. Some **lurk** in famous hotels. Others haunt the grounds where their bodies are buried. Beware of the dark—you may not be alone!

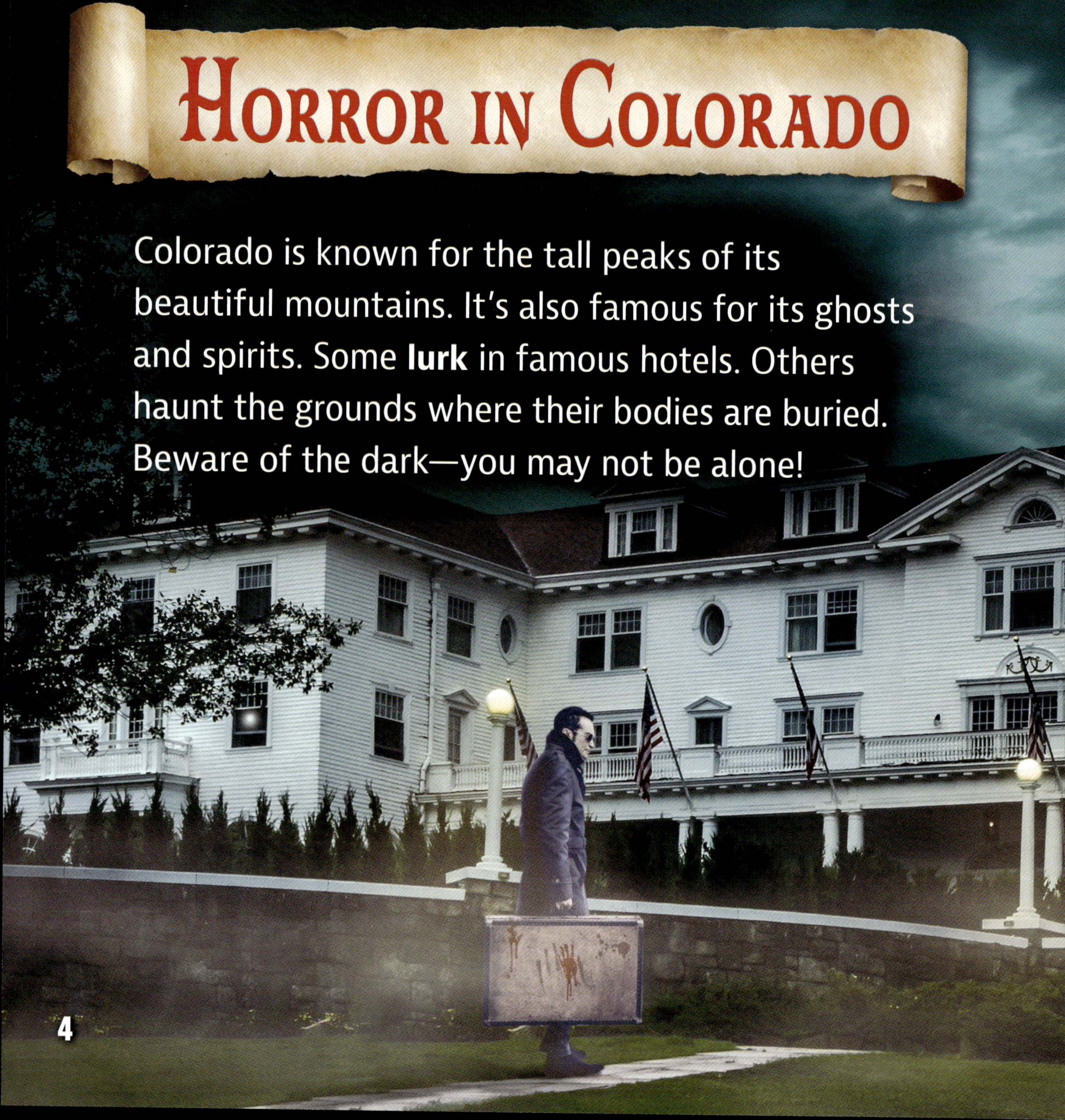

Get ready to read four terrifying tales about Colorado. Turn the page . . . if you dare.

# Bones Below

**Cheesman Park, Denver**

The beautiful Cheesman Park sits in central Denver. People walk their dogs and stroll among the trees and gardens. But below the grounds lie the bones of long-dead residents.

In the 1850s, a large cemetery was created in the city. Years later, the town decided to make the land into a park. Residents were asked to move the remains of loved ones. But many bodies were never moved!

Grave markers in the old cemetery

It is estimated that more than 2,000 of the 5,000 original bodies remain buried in Cheesman Park today.

Cheesman Park

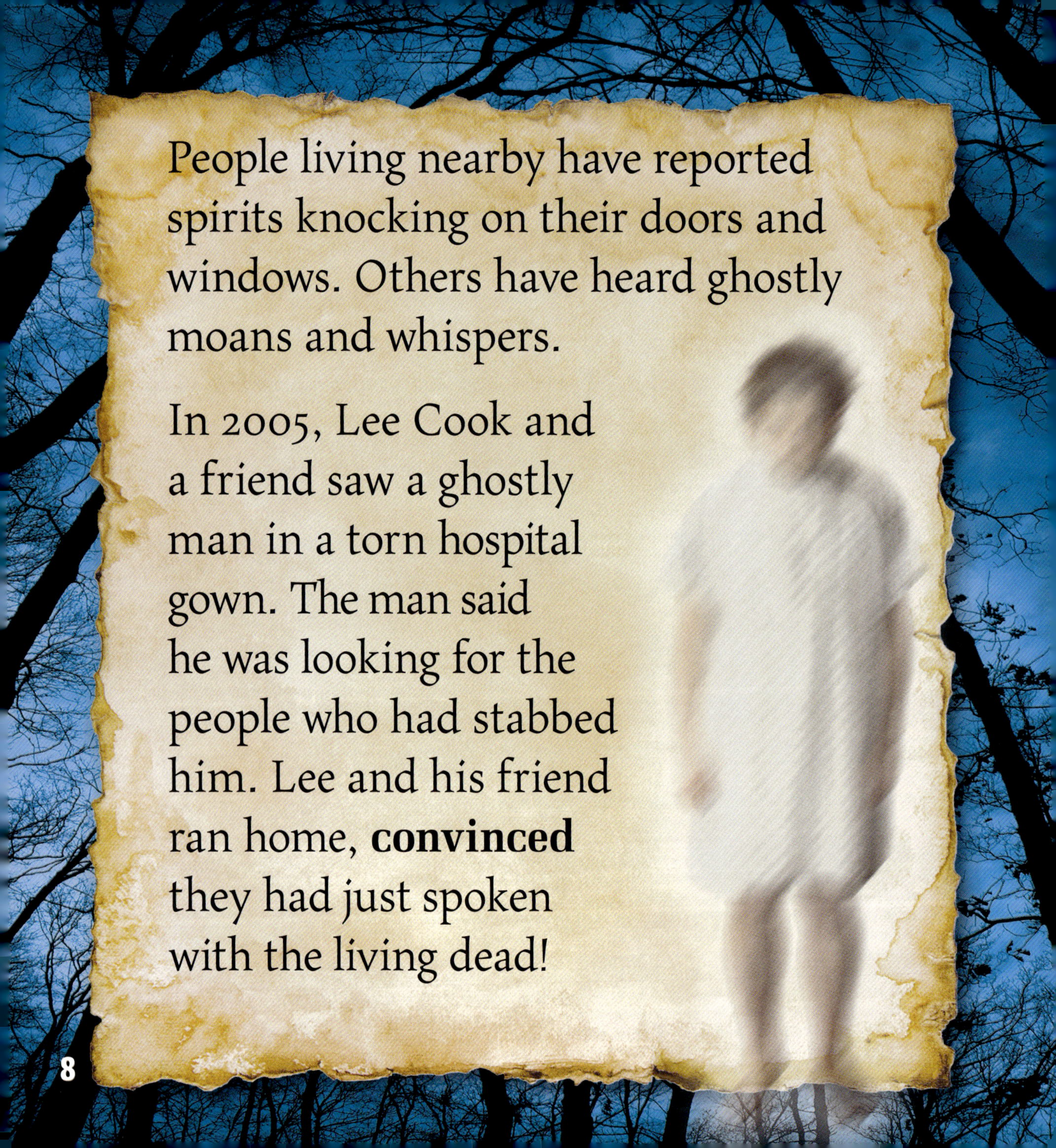

People living nearby have reported spirits knocking on their doors and windows. Others have heard ghostly moans and whispers.

In 2005, Lee Cook and a friend saw a ghostly man in a torn hospital gown. The man said he was looking for the people who had stabbed him. Lee and his friend ran home, **convinced** they had just spoken with the living dead!

Cheesman Park

# Ghostly Globes

**Silver Cliff Cemetery, Silver Cliff**

Outside the old mining town of Silver Cliff lies a small cemetery. **Tombstones** mark the graves. On certain nights, however, something else can be seen—floating lights!

In 1969, a magazine reporter wrote about "dim, round spots of blue-white light" that glowed among the graves.

Legends around the world tell of similar spooky lights, known as will-o'-the-wisps. These glowing **orbs** are thought to be fairies and spirits trying to lead travelers astray.

SILVER CLIFF
CEMETERY
CONDUCT OF PERSONS
WITHIN THE CEMETERY

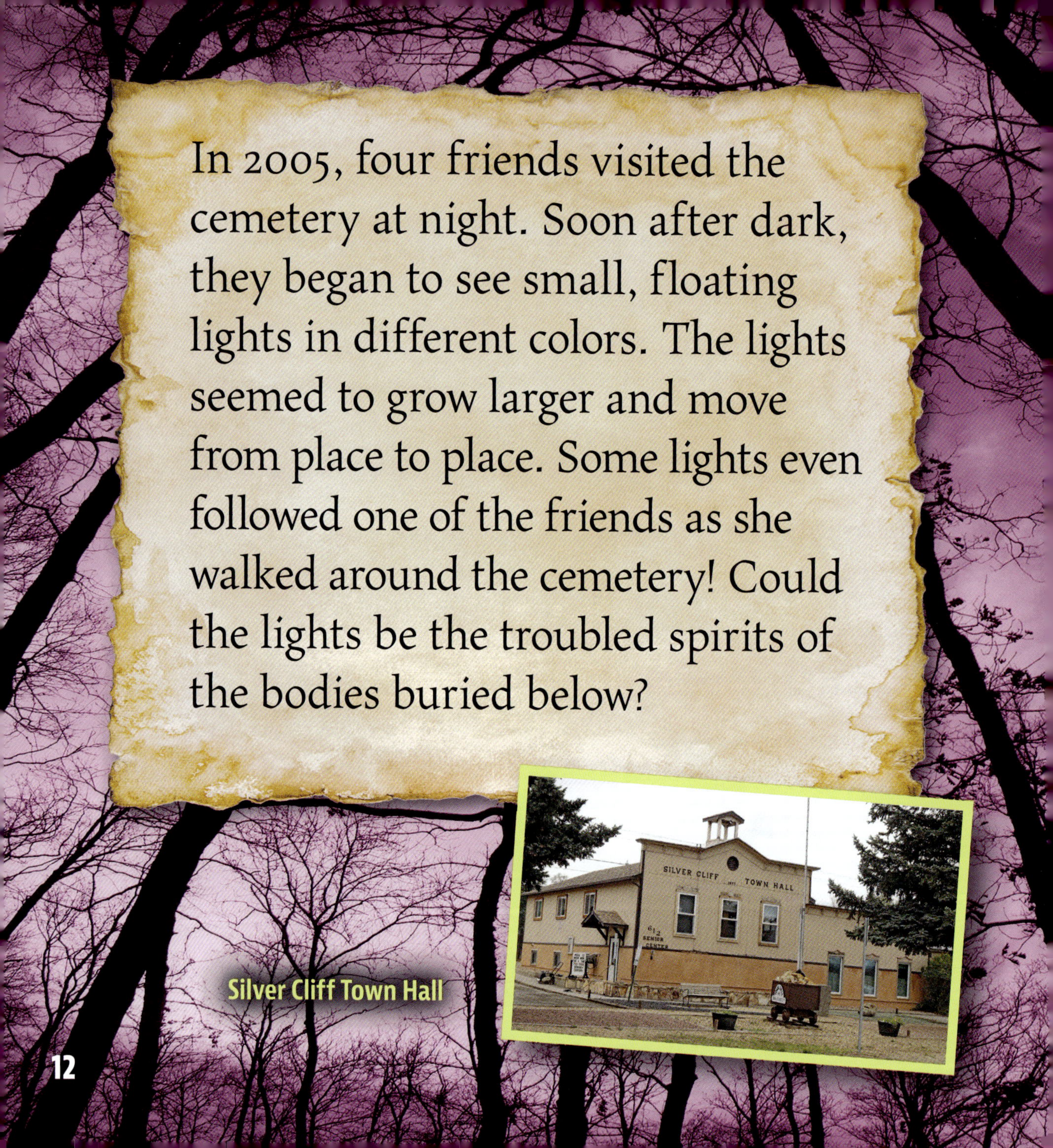


In 2005, four friends visited the cemetery at night. Soon after dark, they began to see small, floating lights in different colors. The lights seemed to grow larger and move from place to place. Some lights even followed one of the friends as she walked around the cemetery! Could the lights be the troubled spirits of the bodies buried below?

Silver Cliff Town Hall

# HORROR HOTEL

## The Stanley Hotel, Estes Park

The Stanley Hotel's excellent service and stunning views draw people from around the world. What many find there, however, is very **otherworldly**.

The Stanley Hotel

The hotel was built more than 100 years ago by Freelan Oscar Stanley and his wife, Flora. For years, guests have claimed to see ghosts of the couple. Freelan is said to appear during tours of the hotel. In the ballroom, Flora has been seen playing the piano.

Freelan and Flora Stanley

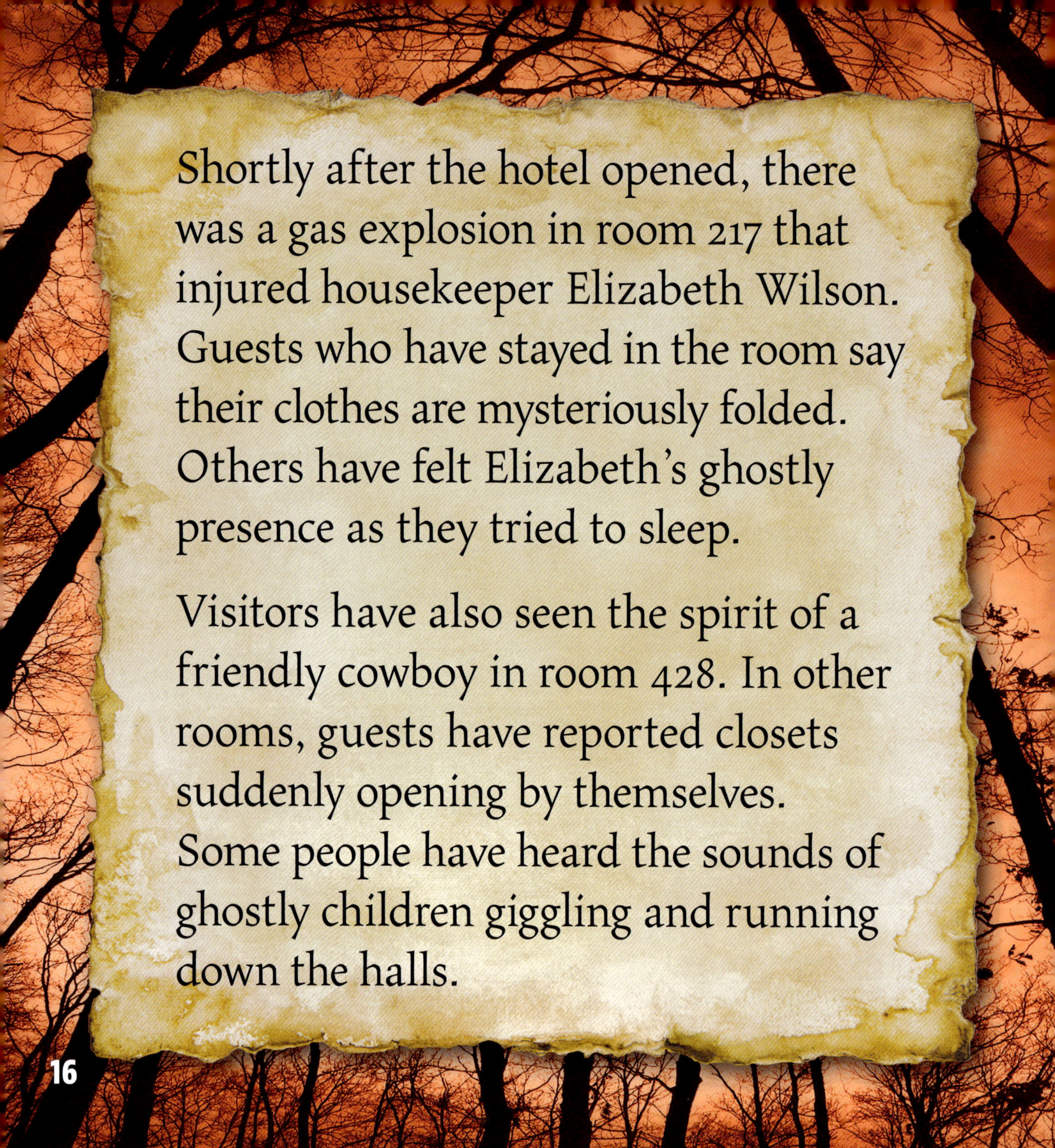

Shortly after the hotel opened, there was a gas explosion in room 217 that injured housekeeper Elizabeth Wilson. Guests who have stayed in the room say their clothes are mysteriously folded. Others have felt Elizabeth's ghostly presence as they tried to sleep.

Visitors have also seen the spirit of a friendly cowboy in room 428. In other rooms, guests have reported closets suddenly opening by themselves. Some people have heard the sounds of ghostly children giggling and running down the halls.

The Stanley Hotel was the **inspiration** for the bestselling novel *The Shining*. In the book, a family is haunted by ghosts in an **isolated** hotel. Later, a movie based on the novel was also released.

# BRIDGE OF DOOM

**The Third Bridge, near Aurora**

In the 1860s, the U.S. Army attacked a Native American village after claiming members of the village killed a young family living near Denver. The army murdered as many as 500 people.

Not far from the **tragic** site is the Third Bridge. For years this area has been known for sad accidents, ghostly sights, and strange sounds. Are the restless spirits of those killed long ago refusing to leave?

The Third Bridge is also known as Ghost Bridge.

Native American and U.S. Army representatives in 1864 before the massacre

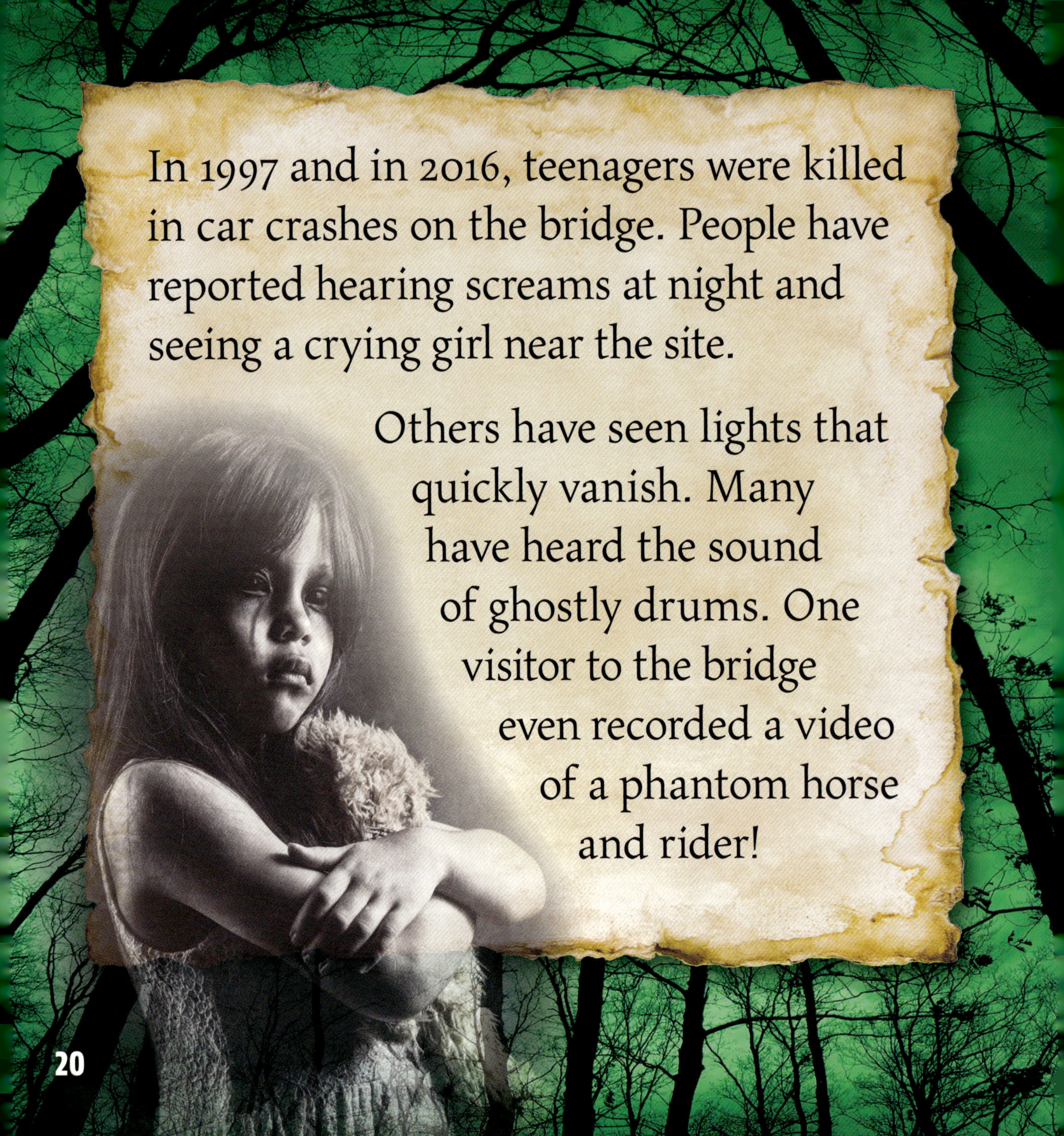

In 1997 and in 2016, teenagers were killed in car crashes on the bridge. People have reported hearing screams at night and seeing a crying girl near the site.

Others have seen lights that quickly vanish. Many have heard the sound of ghostly drums. One visitor to the bridge even recorded a video of a phantom horse and rider!

# Spooky Spots in Colorado

**The Stanley Hotel**
Check into a frightening experience.

**Cheesman Park**
Learn about the bones buried below.

**Silver Cliff Cemetery**
What are those floating, ghostly globes?

**The Third Bridge**
Visit a bridge haunted by the past.



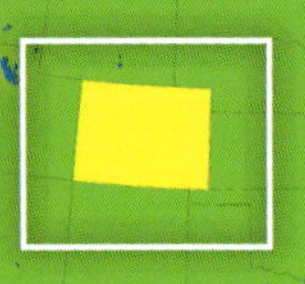

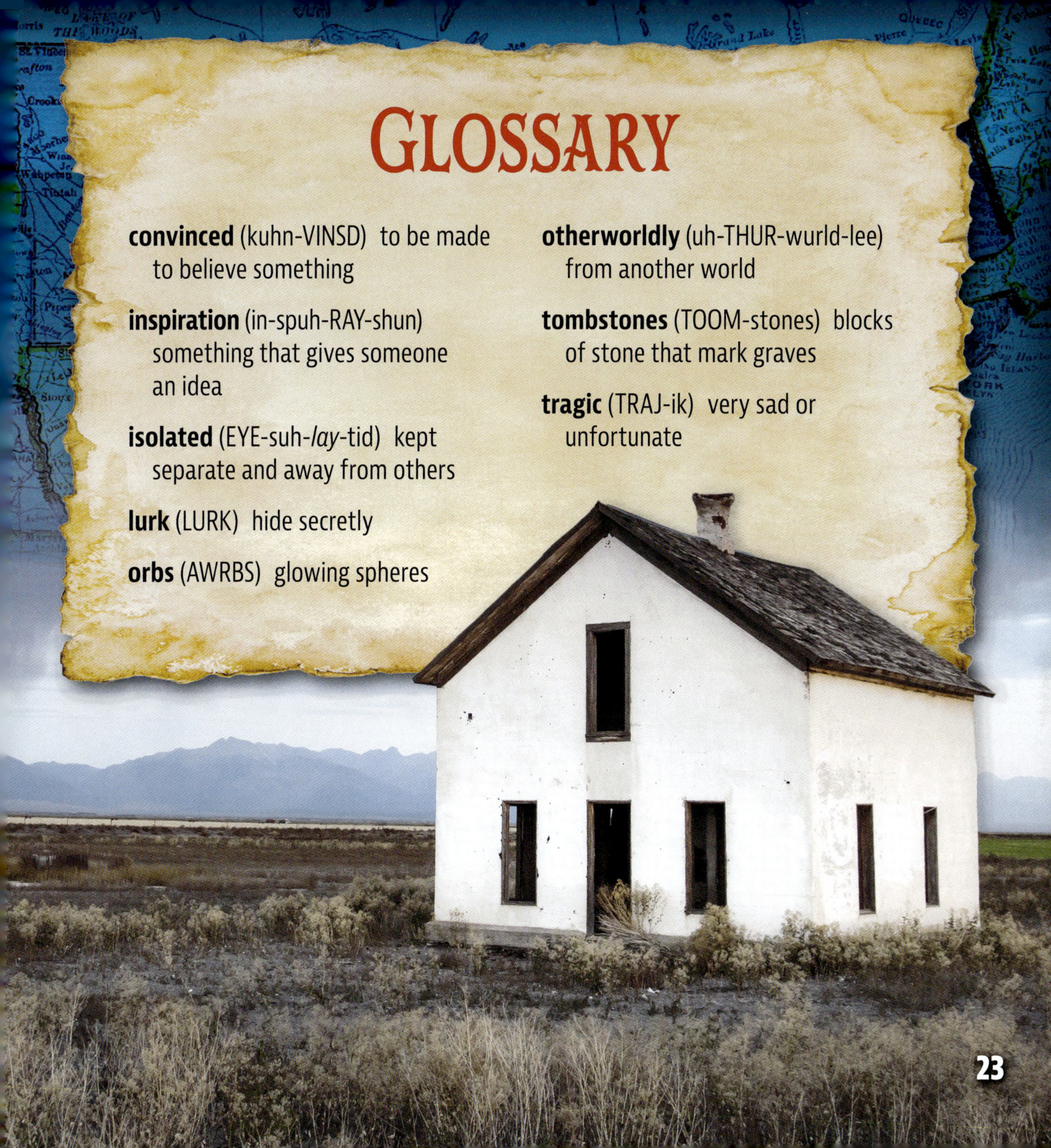

# Glossary

**convinced** (kuhn-VINSD) to be made to believe something

**inspiration** (in-spuh-RAY-shun) something that gives someone an idea

**isolated** (EYE-suh-*lay*-tid) kept separate and away from others

**lurk** (LURK) hide secretly

**orbs** (AWRBS) glowing spheres

**otherworldly** (uh-THUR-wurld-lee) from another world

**tombstones** (TOOM-stones) blocks of stone that mark graves

**tragic** (TRAJ-ik) very sad or unfortunate

# 

INDEX



## Read More

**Markovics, Joyce.** *Chilling Cemeteries (Tiptoe Into Scary Places).* New York: Bearport (2017).

**Phillips, Dee.** *Nightmare in the Hidden Morgue (Cold Whispers II).* New York: Bearport (2017).

## Learn More Online

1. Go to **www.factsurfer.com**
2. Enter "**Horror in Colorado**" into the search box.
3. Click on the cover of this book to see a list of websites.

## About the Author

Spencer Brinker loves to tell "dad jokes" and play word games with his twin girls.